Snoopy's

GRAND SLAM

Snoopy's

GRAND SLAM

Charles M. Schulz

Creative Development Corporation / Holt, Rinehart and Winston

**To Bing Crosby, whose invitation to play in his
great tournament each year inspired these cartoons.**

Published simultaneously in Canada
by Holt, Rinehart and Winston of Canada, Limited.

ISBN: 0-03-002946-5

Library of Congress Catalog Card Number: 72-82150

First Edition

Designer: Craven & Evans / Creative Graphics

Printed in the United States of America

The Crosby

The Masters

The Open